PLAY WITH PAPER

by Thea Bank-Jensen

Having fun with paper is the first and last intention of this book—encouraging children to feel free to experiment, to throw things away if necessary and then begin anew—just for the pleasure of playing with paper! Introduced hundreds of years ago in China, paper cutting and sculpture have a fascinating history, and with the advent of the mobile have become more and more popular in Western culture. Here are simple instructions in words and pictures for making a heat-mobile, troll cats and airplanes, a circus, paper mosaics, paper lace, a helicopter and many more. "Let's play with paper!"

6 and up

study of the difficult child and playground and free activity. Her emphasis is always on inventive fun, leaving the child free to explore the creative possibilities within himself.

PLAY
WITH
PAPER

by

Thea Bank-Jensen

THE MACMILLAN COMPANY   NEW YORK   1962

Original title: Leg Med Papir
Translated from the Danish
by Virginia Allen Jensen

First Printing

The Macmillan Company, New York
Brett-Macmillan Ltd., Galt, Ontario

Printed in the United States of America

18916

CONTENTS

Play with Paper is the title of this book. Those who thumb through its pages will see that the emphasis is on the joy in playing. This is not a collection of model projects for you to copy laboriously because the last thing I want to be is a taskmaster.

The book is intended to encourage your desire to play and create, and to demonstrate how paper can be used for this purpose.

Paper has been in use for hundreds of years. It was introduced originally by a Chinese official named Tsai Lun about the time of Christ's birth. Besides using paper for written communication, the Chinese saw in it a means for artistic expression. Among other things, they made beautiful paper cuttings. The tissue paper was placed in several layers on glass, and a sharp knife was used to cut out patterns, landscapes, animals, and people. These cuttings were used to tell stories, for decoration in homes, for embroidery patterns, and as gifts. The animals and plants had symbolic meaning just as they did earlier in our culture.

The symbolism in the cuttings saved many words for the Chinese. A veil tail, for example, expressed the wish for "great wealth." In Chinese a veil tail is called "tjin yü" and "yü," besides meaning fish, signifies flood. Since the veil tail is a gold fish, it stands for a flood of gold or wealth.

Chinese paper cutting.

The wealthy mandarin and the coolie.

Pictured here is an old illustration for the story of the wealthy mandarin who forgot the poor coolie. It is done with tissue paper cuttings.

Even though paper was first produced about the time of Christ's birth, it was not introduced in Europe until approximately A.D. 1200, after passing circuitously through Samarkand and Arabia to Italy and Spain.

In Europe men discovered how to write and print on paper, and eventually they found that it could be cut with a sharp-edged tool. Scissors were first used for cutting toward the end of the fourteenth century, when they were developed almost in the same form we know today.

Paper cutting or scoring develops special abilities in an individual. In contrast to drawing where it is possible to use many details, the concentration in paper cutting is centered on the whole form and the outlines. The cutter observes the form and expresses that form first and foremost. If he uses colored paper, he represents the flat colors without shading, and he decides which color dominates and characterizes the subject to be portrayed. Paper cutting, using one or several colors, makes possible an artistic growth that demands less time than drawing and painting.

In Europe a technique similar to that used for Chinese paper cutting is still employed in fold art. For example, in Poland people are fond of decorating their walls with glossy paper cuttings, which are used also for window pictures, finely decorated boxes, and many other things.

Fold cutting is an easy and popular technique. Hans Christian Andersen amused himself playing with fold cuttings and he delighted others with the charming designs he made. One of his cuttings is pictured below.

Silhouettes (black on white) were very popular in the seventeenth and eighteenth centuries. They were used especially for portraits. This technique depends entirely upon capturing the character of the subject in profile, since only the outline can be discerned. Designs cut in black or bright colors and mounted on white give particularly sharp effects.

The Chinese have the oldest tradition in paper folding. Many of the folds we make today are of Chinese origin. The Chinese have always been able to play and have a rare ability for using all of their senses in living. They have been able to see, enjoy, and express nature. In our culture today we have too little time for play, too little time to observe and experience. Everything we do must be expedient and rational, and we forget that the pleasure in creating, simply for the experience itself, is an essential part of living.

If this little book develops in some people, children as well as adults, the desire to play with paper; if it encourages them to try things out, to throw things away and begin anew just for pleasure and amusement, it is worth while. Have fun!

P.S. In the last chapter you will find some technical tips about materials which are useful to know before you begin.

One of Hans Christian Andersen's fold cuttings, at the museum in Odense, Denmark. Other fold cuttings by Andersen are on permanent display at the main branch of the New York Public Library, New York City.

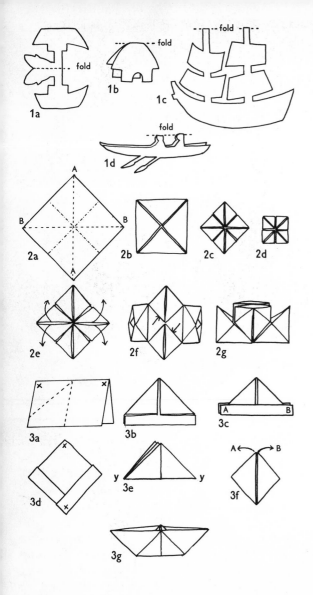

THE GREAT OCEAN

Picture yourself afloat on the great ocean, sailing or steaming along in a vessel that's all your own. You can vary those pictured here, or you can design your own. The methods and a few explanations are here:

Double cutting is used for the island hut, the steamer, the rowboat, and the schooner. Fold heavy paper or oak tag in half. Draw the ship or the hut on the paper so that the outline of the top of the figure coincides with the fold. Then cut out the figure, being careful not to cut it at the fold. When the figure is cut out, it should stand up by itself, being held together at the top along the fold. (See drawings 1a, b, c, and d.)

The steamer is an old Chinese fold which even our great-grandmothers knew. It is made in this way: Use a square piece of paper (on page 47 you will find an easy way to make a square) and make a center fold in each direction by bringing the opposite sides together and creasing along the center. Open the paper and make two diagonal folds by bringing the opposite corners (A-A and B-B) together. Open the paper again and it will be creased like Figure 2a. Now fold all four corners to the center (2b) and crease the folds with your nail. Turn the paper over and fold the corners in to the center again (2c). Turn the paper over and fold the four corners to the center for the third time (2d). Turn the paper once more so that it looks like Figure 2e. Open the ''pockets'' marked with arrows, fold them out, and crease the edges well (2f). Insert

Many kinds of ships sail the ocean. The inhabitants of this little island are out in their boat.

your index fingers in the folds marked by arrows —as far in as possible—and pull out to the sides. As you pull on these folds, the funnels of the steamer will rise to position (2g).

The little boat at the far right is also made with a long-established fold. It is made from a *soldier's hat*. Let's begin with the hat: Using a rectangular piece of paper mark the center by bringing the opposite, long sides together. Then fold the paper in half the other direction (3a) and fold the two corners (x) in to the center

crease (3b). "Lock" these folds by turning the free edges up to the front and the back, and the hat is finished (3c). If you want to make a boat, open the hat and press the two ends A and B against each other so that it looks like Figure 3d. Turn the bottom corners up to the front and the back to meet the point at the top, and then open the newly formed hat, pressing the points (y) against each other, just as you did before. Pull the points A and B out to the left and the right, and the boat is finished.

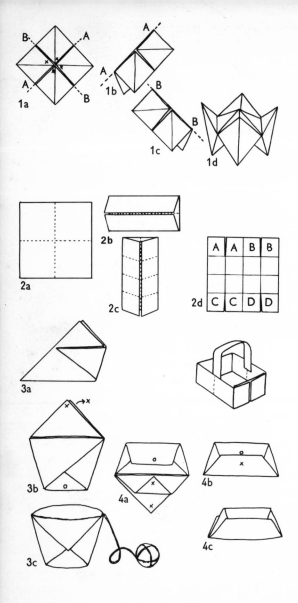

A FEW EASY FOLDS

If you can fold the steamer, you'll find the cootie catcher, the nut cups, and the troll very easy. They are made in the same way except for the last fold. Follow the explanation on page 6 until you have completed Figure 2c, which appears again on this page as Figure 1a. This is the model for all three forms. Fold A to A and B to B as shown in Figures 1b and 1c, and crease the fold well each time. In doing this the four flaps marked (x) will open slightly so that you can slip your fingers underneath them. Push your fingers down to the bottom of the four pockets and press your fingers together. There you have the nut cups (1d). You can play with them or decorate your table with them. When you have your fingers in the cups you will discover quickly that you can open and close them in two directions, so that you have two different mouthlike openings on the underside.

To make a troll, paint one mouth opening red and paint eyes on the flaps. To make a flea or cootie catcher, draw small "flea" dots inside one mouth with pen or pencil. When you are catching "fleas," place your thumb and first three fingers in the cups, open the blank or "empty" mouth and place it in the hair of the "victim." Snap the empty mouth closed; open the "flea" mouth and show off your big catch! People who have never seen this trick before will certainly be surprised and maybe even fooled, if you're fast enough.

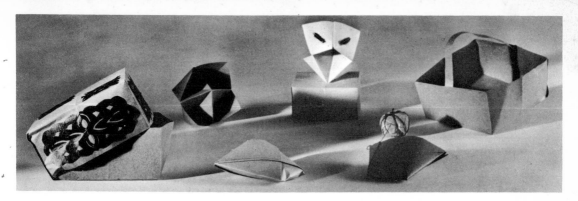

Baskets and boxes are attractive decorated with paper cuttings.

The basket is made with a "16 fold" in the following manner: Use a square piece of paper. Make a center fold in each direction (2a). Open the paper and fold two opposite edges in just to the center line. Open the paper and repeat the fold in the opposite direction. Now you have 16 small squares. Cut the paper at four points (2d), making each cut just one square deep. Paste the basket together, A on A, B on B, etc., and finish it by attaching a handle.

Make the box in the same manner. You will need two squares of paper, one slightly larger than the other, one for the lid and one for the bottom.

The *drinking cup* is also made with a square sheet of paper. In this case you fold one corner to the opposite corner, a diagonal fold. Fold the right point over to the left, the cut edge parallel to the fold at the bottom; fold the left corner over to the right, as shown in Diagram 3a. Finally turn the top points marked (x) down in the front and in the back. This makes a very good drinking cup, useful especially on a hike (3c). You can use this cup for playing ball too, as you will see in the picture above. Roll thin paper (tissue paper, for example) into a ball and bind it with yarn (it must not be heavy). Fasten the ball to the cup with fine steel wire or string. Swing the ball up and try to catch it in the cup. It takes practice. Try it!

If you make the drinking cup large enough, using paper 20″ by 20″ it becomes a fine hat. Make it in this way: Fold the cup as far as Figure 3b. Turn the cup upside down so that the points are toward you. Fold the bottom of the cup (o) down over most of one of the sides and turn up one of the points (x) as in Figure 4a. Turn the other point (x) up on the other side. Now turn the last two folds up once again toward (o), Figure 4b, and your hat is ready to wear (4c).

For this and other hats, you can use newspaper or heavy wrapping paper.

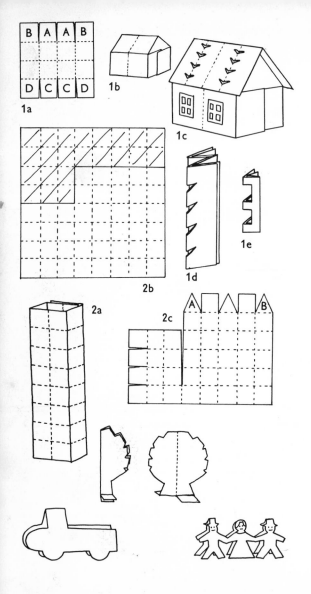

HOUSES AND TREES IN THE CITY

It's fun to make a city with its variety of houses and buildings. Here are a few suggestions: The house pictured at the far right is made from a simple "16" fold by cutting three slits in two opposite edges with a scissors (1a). Then glue flap A over A, and flap C over C to form the roof; then glue B halfway over B, and D halfway over D to form the ends of the house (1b). The house next to this one was made in the same way, except that an extra piece of paper was cut to fit the roof and extend over the sides of the house. You can make a more elaborate roof by folding the paper in fourths and snipping out notches on the folds (1d). Unfold the roof and glue it on the house. The windows are made from smaller pieces of paper, folded in the same manner, but cut as in Figure 1e.

The church and the tall building are made with a double "16 fold." That is, each of the 16 squares is marked off in four quarters by folding the paper once more in each direction, making 64 squares altogether. For the skyscraper use all the squares (2a), and form the roof by cutting down two squares from the top at the four corners and folding them over.

To make the church cut away some of the squares as shown in Figure 2b, and cut the remaining squares to look like Figure 2c. Glue the church tower together, A over B. The free end of the nave is glued together in the same way as the small house. Make roofing for the nave and the tower. You can glue on windows

Sunlight floods the city square. Trees, cars, and people appear as if by magic from double cuttings. You'll see how to make them in the drawings at the left.

and doors like those in the picture. Trees, and people are easy to make with double cut-

tings. See the drawings at the left and in the next chapter.

A FARMYARD, THE PEOPLE AND ANIMALS

Perhaps it's a gloomy day. You are thinking of summer. Suddenly you are filled with the desire to see a farm in sunny country-side. With your scissors and some oak tag or heavy paper you can create a farm with the farmer and his wife, the buildings, and all the farmyard animals. You'll be surprised to see how quickly it all takes shape.

Maybe the animals don't look like real animals, but for you, the cutter and creator, they are *exactly* right.

Simply draw the figures on a piece of paper folded in half, making sure that all the drawings run along the edge of the fold at some point. When you are cutting out the figure be *sure* you don't cut the folded edge. The cut figures stand up because they are hinged at the fold.

The wife in the picture, however, is made in another way. Fold the paper lengthwise and cut only half the figure (1a). When you open it up the figure is whole (1b). Then cut off one side of the kerchief to make her face. She will keep her balance easily if you cut a narrow strip along the edge of her skirt (starting at the x in Figure 1a) and push the strip back as a support (1c).

The fence is made from a double folded strip, folded in half once again (2a). Cut it as shown in the drawing. Be careful not to cut the points of the pickets! (2b).

Evergreen trees are made by cutting the pattern from two pieces of paper laid together

The farm, the people, and the animals are cut from red oak tag. Many figures can be made from a single sheet of oak tag.

(3a and 3b). Make a slit halfway up the center of one piece and cut from the top halfway down the other. Slip the first half down over the second and the tree will stand (3c).

All these techniques are suitable for many other things. You can make a zoo, a city, a market. For additional color and character you can draw and paint on the figures.

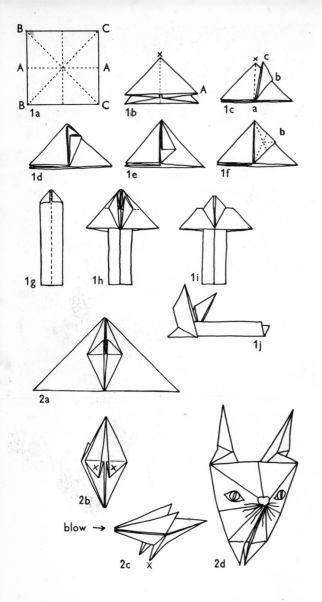

1a 1b 1c 1d 1e 1f 1g 1h 1i 1j 2a 2b 2c blow 2d

AIRPLANES AND TROLL-CATS

Here is an airplane which requires some dexterity, but flies very well. Follow each step carefully. Use a square piece of paper. Fold it diagonally, first in one direction and then the other. Open the paper and make a center fold in each direction (1a). Now bring A to A, B to B, and C to C as shown in Figure 1b. Lay the paper flat on the table with the apex marked x pointing away from you. The point at the right, marked A in Figure 1b should be folded up to point x. Crease the fold with your nail and don't open this fold again. Now we have reached Figure 1c. Fold side a-b in to the center fold (1d); open this fold and fold side b-c in to the center fold (1e). Open this fold; grasp point (b) and press together the folds on either side of b (marked in Figure 1f) with the thumb and middle finger. Turn this point in toward the center line and press down so that a sail-like piece is left standing. Now press the sail toward the nose of the plane and fold it down flat. Repeat the same folds on the left side.

Cut a long rectangular piece of paper for the tail and make a point at the top with the fold shown in 1g, so that it will fit inside the wing piece (1h). Fold the nose of the plane back along the dotted line (Figures 1h and 1i). Give the entire plane a good hard fold along the center line (Figure 1j) and let it fly. If it dips to the ground the nose is too heavy, and you must make a longer, and possibly wider tail.

14

You can draw eyes and whiskers on the troll-cat so that it really looks like one.

The *troll-cat* is made like the airplane as far as Figure 2a. Flip the paper over and fold the two sides (the wings) in the same manner as you did the other side. This time you do not press the two sails down. Hold onto the two sails (marked x in Figure 2b) and blow in the open end of the figure as hard as you can (2c). There, you have the cat just as you see it in Figure 2d.

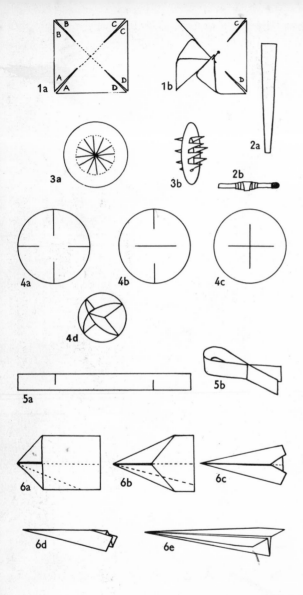

1a 1b 2a 3a 3b 2b 4a 4b 4c 4d 5a 5b 6a 6b 6c 6d 6e

PLAYING IN THE SUN AND WIND

Wind toys are fun. When the wind catches one and whirls away with it, you'll have a real "race with the wind" to catch the toy again.

The *windmill* is the tamest wind toy. It doesn't fly away, it simply whirls around. It is made from a square piece of oak tag. First, fold two diagonals and mark the center. Cut on the diagonal from all four corners halfway to the middle (1a). Use a piece of steel wire and fasten a bead at one end. Draw the other end through one of each of the points A, B, C, and D (1b), and finally through the center of the square. Thread another bead or two on the wire and twist the free end around a slender stick. The windmill is completed. If the oak tag is a different color on each side, you'll have a "whirl" of many colors.

If you don't have any beads you can make them easily. Cut a triangular piece of paper, approximately 8 inches high and 3 inches at the base (Figure 2a). Roll this, starting at the base, tightly around a knitting needle or a matchstick (2b), and glue the end in place. Remove the needle or stick and the bead is ready for use. It will last longer if you lacquer it.

For the *wind wheel* use a circular piece of oak tag. Draw a smaller circle inside this and divide it into eight or twelve pieces (3a). From the center outward cut on the division lines. Fold the pieces out, alternately, first to one side and then to the other. Set the wind wheel on the

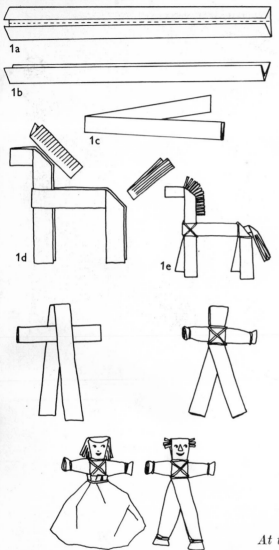

sidewalk or on the beach and away it rolls.

The *wind ball* rolls just as fast as the wind wheel, but is more difficult to make. Use three identical circles of oak tag (it must be flexible) about 4 to 6 inches in diameter. Cut slits in the circles as shown in the drawings (4a-b-c) and fit the pieces together. Begin by folding circle 4a in half and slipping it through the center slit of circle 4b. Ease circle 4a to the right so the outer edges meet perpendicularly and gently open circle 4a. Carefully draw circle 4c over them, moving the circles cautiously until all the slits are fitted in the proper places and the wind ball is complete (4d).

The *helicopter* flies best when you start it from a window or other high point. It is made from one strip of paper or oak tag about 4 inches long. Near each end of the strip make a slit as in Figure 5a. Lock the two ends together as in Figure 5b. Toss it into the air and watch it whirl about.

The *airplane* is drawn on page 16. Use a rectangular piece of paper. Make a center fold the length of the paper. At one end fold the two corners into the center fold (6a). Now fold the slanted sides into the center fold and along the dotted line (Figure 6a) so that you achieve Figure 6b. Similarly fold the slanted sides once again along the dotted line (seen in 6b) to make Figure 6c. Now make a sharp center fold (6d) and the plane is ready for take-off (6e). It glides beautifully and never fails.

At the left are a man and his wife on their way to the field to bring the horses home. Just like their animals, seen in the photograph on the next page, they are made of folded paper strips.

HORSES IN THE FIELD

Animals of folded paper strips can be varied. Here is the basic model for horses. But dogs, cats, giraffes, lions and many other animals are made by the same method.

Fold two long pieces of paper as shown in the drawings 1a and 1b on the opposite page. Fold them in half (1c). Fold one strip for the body and hind legs, and the other for the head, neck, and forelegs. Bind the two pieces together with a crisscross, or staple them together. They can be fastened with a clip or glued just as well. The mane and tail are cut as shown in Figures 1d and 1e.

Using the same technique you can make a man, as you see in the drawing, and if you want a woman, simply make a skirt of tissue or crepe paper.

With imagination and color, you'll find endless possibilities for variation on these basic figures.

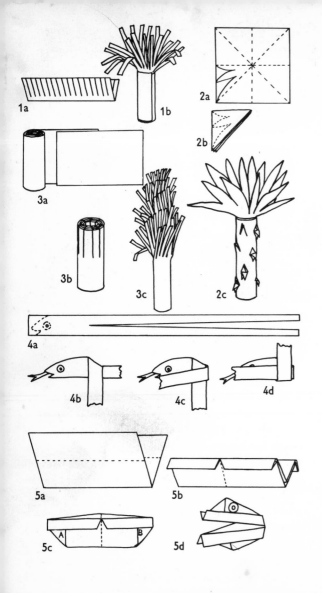

ANIMALS AND TREES OF THE JUNGLE

Here is just a sampling of the many kinds of trees you can make. The leaves of the palm tree in the center of the photograph are made by folding a long piece of paper over once and cutting it like the teeth of a comb (1a). Then it is rolled and inserted into the trunk, a piece of paper rolled into a cylinder and glued (1b).

The leaves of the other two palms are made from squares of paper, folded (2a) and cut as in Figure 2b. Before you insert them in the trunk draw each leaf carefully over a scissors or pencil, curling it. The trunk of tree 2c has notches cut in it.

The *pull palm* is made with several pieces of paper cut the same size and rolled into a tube. The center of the tube must be large enough to accommodate a scissors. Begin with a single sheet of paper, roll it halfway, and lay the next piece on it; continue rolling until the second sheet is half rolled. Continue until you have four or five layers. Glue the last edge in place so the roll won't come undone (3a). These palms are especially handsome if you use several different shades of green paper. When the roll is finished, cut down 1/3 the length of the roll at one end (3b). The more slits you make, the finer and more handsome the leaves will be. Finally and carefully, ease and pull the paper up from the center of the roll. Turn the roll slightly as you pull, and the palm grows tall and luxuriant (3c). Be careful not to pull too much out at a time because it will fall apart

if you do. Trees are fun to make and you can grow a whole forest in no time. Sometime try making the roll with full-sized newspaper sheets. The tree will shoot up like Jack's magic beanstalk.

For the *crocodile* and the *snake* use strips of paper about 20–30″ long and 3/4 to 1″ wide. Fold the strip in half lengthwise and slit the back on the fold up to the head (4a). Then start making the Jacob's ladder fold. The Jacob's ladder fold is made by folding one strip over and on top of the other, alternating strips as you go (4b-c-d). The crocodile's legs are made

in the same way, and they are pasted on the finished body. The head is pasted on as well. To make the head use a square of paper. Fold it in half (5a) and turn the long sides in toward the center fold, creasing on the dotted line so that each half is divided lengthwise once again. Fold the two newly formed edges out and down on each side. Find the center of each side and clip a notch at both center points (5b). Turn the two corners, A and B, in under the last folds (5c). There you have a "boat" which you fold prow to stern and the croc's mouth is completed.

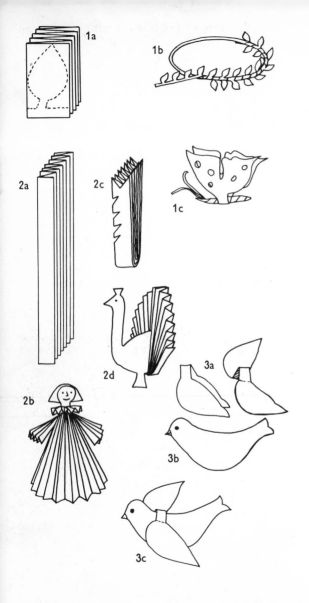

A MOBILE ENLIVENS YOUR HOME

A room has a life and color of its own when graced with the quiet animation of a mobile. It's fun to make them in the first place, and then it's fun to watch them. Mobiles can be symmetrical or asymmetrical. They can be made of cardboard, paper, reed, feathers, metal, etc. Here are two suggestions using paper and reed.

The *butterfly mobile* is made by entwining a ring of reed with a strip of paper, cut as leaves (1a). A careful hand is used in wrapping the leaves about the previously bound ring of reed, and the end of the leaf strip is glued in place (1b). The butterflies in the photograph are cut from white typing paper, the wings for

The *peacock tail* is made with the same accordian-pleated fold (2a) except that the folded paper is bent over double and glued together in the middle (2c). If you give it a few snips as in the drawing, the tail will be even more elegant. The peacock's body is cut from oak tag (2d). The bird in flight is made according to the drawings (3a-b-c).

The *elephant* is made entirely of Jacob's ladder strips, except for the tusks and ears, which are cut from oak tag. The mobile figures hang from thin wooden knitting needles bound together, and they move easily in the air.

Mobiles are living toys. Suspend them from the ceiling or any light fixture. You will enjoy watching their shadow movements. If you get tired of a mobile, you can throw it away. It's no trouble to make a new one.

each being cut in varied patterns. A matchstick bound in a strip of paper, to which a long thread is fastened, is glued in each set of wings (1c), and the butterflies are hung at different heights. The wings should be curled slightly by drawing them over a pencil so that they wave gracefully as they move about in the air. The feelers are simply made by gluing thin strips of paper to the heads.

The *other mobile* is a man with an accordion-pleated body and Jacob's ladder arms and legs (see page 21), and a lady made from two pieces of accordion-pleated tissue paper. The largest piece is sewed together at one end (the skirt) and the other piece (arms) is sewed in the middle and attached to the top of the skirt. In the photograph the skirt is embellished by a cutout pattern.

DECORATIVE NEWSPAPERS

Someday you may be sitting around feeling rather bored. You can't find anything to play with. But you can always find an old newspaper, and a little yarn or string. Then you'll have all the company you want, people and animals. The drawings at the left show you how to construct the basic forms for both.

Take a single sheet of newspaper and roll it the long way into a cylinder and crush it the full length so that it stays rolled. If you roll it too tightly, the cylinder will break when you try to bend it. Then take half a sheet of newspaper and roll it the short way into a cylinder. Twist both cylinders lightly with your hands. With the longer cylinder form a loop and place the shorter cylinder between the two "legs," allowing the legs a wide stance. Bind the arms (the shorter cylinder) in place with a crisscross of yarn or string. The loop becomes the head and it can be filled out with a little paper crushed into a ball. Wrap some yarn around the arms and legs and the figure is complete. The figures can be dressed in newspaper, crepe or tissue paper. You can make hats and hair. You can make large and small people. The animals are made with the same type of cylinders and put together as shown in the figures at the left.

To make the people or the animals fatter, crumple small pieces of paper and bind the pieces to the figure where you want to fill it out. Notice the bull in the photograph at the right.

Masks, too, are easy to make from newspapers. In a sheet of newspaper cut out a nose.

A couple of newspapers and a little string are all you need to make this stalwart bullfight scene. Maybe you have an idea for something entirely different.

Then hold the ''mask'' over your face and mark where the eyes and mouth should be with a pencil, and you are ready to cut them out. It's possible to put teeth in the mouth by pasting them on the back of the mask. To make the mask stay on your head, cut out paper strips and attach one on each side of the mask; then fasten them at the back of the head with a paper clip. The mask will be stronger if you cut it out of several layers of newspaper and bind the edges with strips of paper. You can paint masks with different colors and expressions, depending on who you want to be.

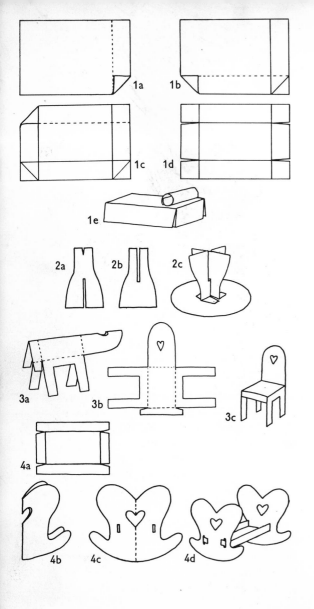

PAPER FURNITURE FOR A DOLL HOUSE

Here is an easy way to furnish your doll house. See for example, the handsome couch the father doll is resting on. It is made from a rectangular piece of thin oak tag. Start by folding the four corners an equal distance toward the center (1a-b-c). Then cut slits at four points (1d) and glue it together just as you did in making the basket on page 8. Finally you furnish the couch with a rolled cushion to make the father comfortable (1e).

The *wardrobe* is made from a 16 fold, cut in the same way as you did the house (page 10, Figure 1a), that is, three slits, one square deep, on two opposite sides. Flap A should be glued to fit exactly over A and flap B over B; glue flaps C and D in the same way.

The *table top* is a circular piece of oak tag, and the table legs are fitted together like the farmer's evergreen was on page 12, Figure 3a-b-c. Cut the two legs exactly alike (2a-b), and slit one to the middle from the top and the other from the bottom. Fit one into the other and fold over an equal amount of the top on each leg. Put glue on these tabs and fasten the legs to the bottom of the table top (2c).

The chairs are made with a double cutting. Draw half the chair on a piece of oak tag folded in half, and cut it out (3a), remembering the slits and notches. In order to make all the chairs the same size, use the first chair as a pattern for the others (3b).

Begin the *cradle* by cutting the rocker ends from a double folded piece of oak tag (4b-c) and cut out the slits and the heart-shaped notch. Then cut a rectangular piece of oak tag with tab-slits at the short ends (4a). The distance between these tabs should correspond to the distance between the slits in the rocker ends. Slip the tabs through the slits and fold them flush with the rocker ends. There is your cradle.

You can furnish an entire doll house this way. The members of the doll family pictured here are small, but they are made just like the newspaper dolls on page 24. In this case the bodies are made from old dress patterns and then clothed. You can fill your house with old dolls and young dolls, happy and sad dolls. Old shoe boxes make excellent houses.

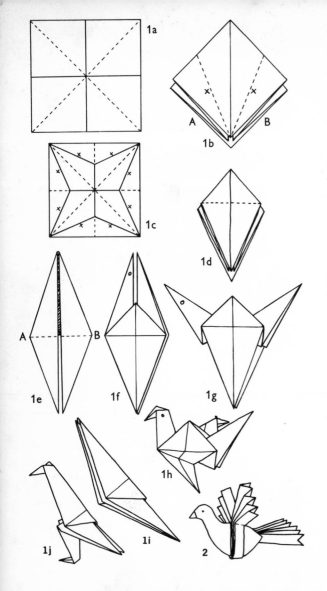

BIRDS THAT WALK AND BIRDS THAT FLY

Festive birds are delightful, for play or decoration, on mobiles or as Christmas ornaments. In the spring they look charming hung on a bouquet of budding branches, and in the dark of winter they are a cheery addition to a spray of greens.

For the *bird at the far right,* one that can flap its wings, use a square sheet of paper. Being sure to open the paper completely after each fold, make a diagonal fold in each direction, and a center fold in each direction (1a). Then fold the paper as shown in Figure 1b, and then fold all layers of sides A and B up to the center fold, along the dotted lines. Now open the entire sheet of paper, lay it flat on the table, and crease toward you along the lines of the last folds you made, so that a four-point star is formed. Press gently at the points marked x in Figure 1c, turning these edges under. Push both sets of opposite corners down and together and lay the figure flat as shown in Figure 1d. Now lift the ends, pointing toward you and fold them up as far as you can (Figure 1e), one to the front and one to the back. Take the point A on top and fold it over to point B as you would turn the pages in a book. Turn the figure over to the reverse side and once again turn the top point A over to B (1f). Grasp the two points at the top in Figure 1f and pull them out to the sides, pressing them down at the angle that a bird's tail and throat should have. Open one of these points (o)

slightly and fold it down for a head. The two flaps hanging down become the wings, and they should be folded obliquely upward, and then down again at the ends as shown in the drawing of the finished bird. If you hold the bird's throat and pull gently on its tail, it will flap its wings.

The *ravens* standing in the picture at the left are made in the same way up to Figure 1f. At this point you should fold the figure in half lengthwise and place it in the position shown in Figure 1i. The two long, thin ends are the tail. The wide point at the left on the inside should be folded down and under as legs which will support the bird. The remaining point is folded down and becomes the raven's head (1j).

The two other birds hovering in the air, are made of wings, beaks, and tails pasted on single bodies, cut in any way you please. In the drawing (2) the wings and tail are made with an accordion-pleated fold. You will find other birds on page 22.

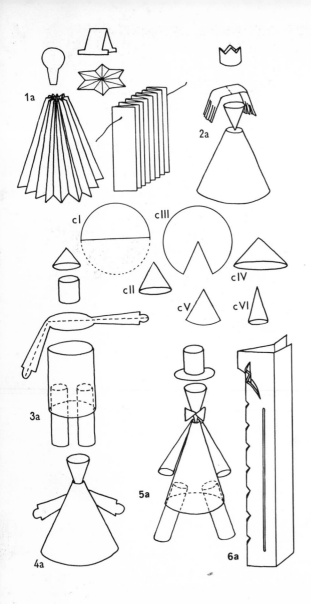

A WEDDING PARTY

It's fun to play even when you don't know what the result of your play will be. The figures pictured at the right are the result of playing with an accordion-pleated paper, cylinders of various heights and diameters, and many different cones.

The *minister* is made from an accordion-pleated piece of paper five times as long as it is wide. A piece of thread is strung through at the neck. The head is cut from a piece of oak tag with a neck long enough to insert in the robe. Before you insert the head, you can make a collar for him with a slit for the neck. The hat is cut from a piece of oak tag folded double. Figure 1a shows the different parts of the minister.

The *bride* is created with a large and a small cone. Cut off the pointed end of the large cone and glue the point of the small cone into the cut end of the large one (2a). (If you form a cone from a half circle of paper [CI], the cone will have the shape of CII. If you remove a pie-shaped piece from a circle as in Figure CIII, the cone will look like Figure CIV. If you form a cone from the pie-shaped piece CV, it will look like CVI.)

The *bridegroom* is made by gluing two long, slender cylinders inside a larger cylinder. A circle of paper is glued on top of the large cylinder and a small cylinder is pasted on this for a head. He is completed by adding a coolie hat, flat arms and shoes, and a pert bow tie. In Figure 3a you can see the separate parts. The *bridesmaid* is made like the bride except that she

has arms (4a). The *best man* is made with both cylinders and cones, and the bride's proud parents are proportioned from cones of varying widths and heights. The father's hat is made by gluing a cylinder on a circle of paper, and his striped trousers are of wrapping paper (5a).

For all these figures, where the gluing area is small, the polyvinyl resin-type glues work very successfully. They dry quickly and adhere well. On page 46 you'll find tips on materials.

The *church window* is a long rectangle of red paper, folded and cut (6a).

The number of wedding party members can be increased to include ring bearers, flower girls, aunts and uncles.

CUTTING AND PASTING WITH COLORED PAPER

Clear, bright colors are inspiring. The greatest pleasure is found in discovering just what it is you want to make, and deciding and choosing for yourself the best colors for the job. In color cutting, particularly, value exists in having as large a choice of beautiful, clear colors as possible. As a rule small children go about this without restraint. It is important not to destroy this spirit as children grow older. You must not expect the things they make to be attractive and exact. The heart of experience in color cutting—as in all other creative work— should always be the pleasure in the work process itself. The demands should come only from within oneself, and should not be imposed from without.

The actual technique of color cutting is very easy. Without making any sketches cut out the desired picture or design. To get the overall effect before gluing, cut out all the pieces, as suggested, and let them lie loose on the background (construction paper, for example). As very young children sometimes have difficulty keeping track of all the pieces, it may be best for them to paste as they cut.

A good gluing method: lay the pieces face down on a newspaper, spreading on the glue with a brush or your finger. Then place the piece, glued-side down, on the background, pressing it down with a clean cloth. The cloth will absorb any excess glue and clean your fingers as well.

All kinds of paper can be used for paper mosaics—glossy paper, cardboard, or wrapping paper. The sad lady below was cut from glossy paper and glued on red cardboard.

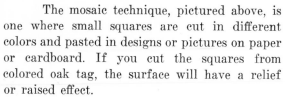

The mosaic technique, pictured above, is one where small squares are cut in different colors and pasted in designs or pictures on paper or cardboard. If you cut the squares from colored oak tag, the surface will have a relief or raised effect.

Sometimes it is amusing to use figured paper, for example, shelf paper, wrapping paper, or wallpaper. There are many possibilities for experiment. Notice the picture on the following page.

Some pieces of colored paper, a little glue, and you can construct pictures that are colorful additions to any wall.

From colored pictures in magazines or catalogues, you can find a variety of shapes, designs and textures. Cut out and put them together. The resulting combinations can be dramatic and often amusing. (See the preceding page.)

TEARING

Instead of cutting the pieces of paper, you can tear out the forms you desire. You can use any type of paper, but of course, paper with designs or color is most effective; newspaper provides excellent variation in pictures, print, and advertising. The form you want may be difficult to achieve at first without a scissors, but you'll learn quickly, and the torn edges will give life to your picture. Glue the pieces on a background, white or colored paper, as you did with ordinary paper cutting. Pick up a piece of paper and the ideas will come —the striped paper is the roof of a house, the polka-dot paper is just right for a child's dress, and from the green paper you'll tear the heavy crown of a tree. You'll discover quickly how many possibilities the different papers have, and what you had been using for packages, news, catalogues, and candy bars will take on new life in the pictures you create. In the picture of the girl under the tree a piece of newspaper is combined with tissue paper and other papers. For the dark-of-night picture of the boy in his sailboat only newspaper has been employed, and it is pasted on black oak tag. Notice how the black-and-white areas of the newspaper are used in the sail.

TISSUE PAPER IN RELIEF

Crumpled tissue paper is an entertaining medium. Tissue paper is easy to mold and generally easy to work with.

The tissue paper should be torn in pieces and crumpled into the shapes you desire. Then glue the pieces liberally on the wrong side (be careful not to get glue too near the edges because the colors run!). Press the paper down carefully with a cloth, which will absorb the excess glue.

You can use tissue paper for tearing as well. Tear the pieces in the forms you want without wrinkling them. Softer outlines are achieved by tearing than by cutting. In addition and for contrast see how well tearing combines with cutting. Try using torn and crumpled tissue paper together.

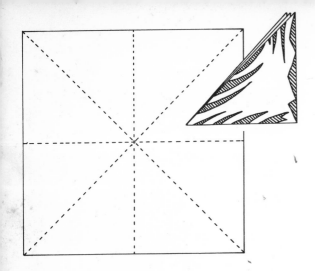

CUTTING PAPER LACE

Cutting paper lace is a fascinating game. Simply fold a piece of paper and cut pieces out of it on the folds; when you open the paper, you'll always be surprised by the variety of design. With some experience you will be able to cut designs according to plan.

The technique is easy. Using a square of paper, fold it in half, and fold it in half once again, forming a quarter square. Fold the small square diagonally so the two folded sides meet and the paper is triangular. Then cut out slits or pieces in different sizes and shapes, first on the folded sides and then on the open edges if you wish. (The cutting you do on the folded sides will be the design at the center of your paper when you open it, and the cutting you do on the open edges will be the border.

Paper lace can be used for table decoration. Even small children can cut it with ease, and grownups can become accomplished. Either white or black paper is suitable and you'll find that colored, glossy paper is lovely when cut in patterns.

You can paste the design on colored paper or wherever it shows to advantage, on a windowpane, for instance. In cutting paper lace the results are almost always different and ever decorative.

Making this design requires a sharp scissors and some careful cutting. The pieces cut out are comparatively large.

Even small children can cut patterns like the one in this picture. Opening the paper is exciting, and always a surprise.

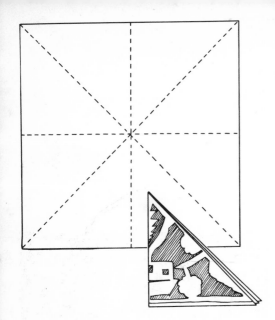

SYMMETRICAL FOLD CUTTING

This play with paper brings pleasure and surprise in multiplication. For example, you fold a square piece of paper in half, first in one direction and then the other. Finally you fold the small square diagonally so that the two folded sides meet (exactly as you did with cutting paper lace on page 36). Then you cut along the edges of the sides formed by folds. The drawing shows houses and trees, and you cut only half of each because they will be whole when you open the paper. You can cut many other figures that are symmetrical. If you choose to cut an asymmetrical figure you must cut it whole at the outer edge and you will have two figures when you open the paper. If you cut the figures out, an outline of them remains in the paper forming a design. This design is called a negative cutting. When the outline is cut away and the forms remain the design is called a positive cutting.

Fold cutting is not just an amusing game with paper and scissors, but is a practical and colorful solution for table and wall decorations. Cuttings glued on contrasting backgrounds are particularly effective. Most light weight paper: typing paper, glossy paper, paper napkins, tissue paper, can be used for fold cutting.

Here is a positive cutting, held together by a solid, narrow border. You can see how it was cut in the drawing on page 38.

The easiest type of fold cutting is probably the negative cutting, where the figures are cut out, and the remaining holes form the design.

SERIES CUTTING

A line of paper dolls holding hands are the figures we usually see in *series cutting*. But series cutting can be used in many other ways, partly for play and partly for celebrating festive occasions; series cuttings make excellent table decorations. Series cutting is easy, as long as you remember that the figures should be attached at several points, so they will actually stand. The figures in the picture are made from thin oak tag; and using this, up to six figures can be cut at one time. If you try to cut more layers than this, the figures will slip about and the edges will fray.

The trees, the children, and the birds in the picture are cut like those in the drawing. Notice in particular how they are connected. It is essential for good balance that the figures be attached at the proper places. Try yourself to create new figures. Possibilities are unlimited!

Series cuttings are entertaining decorations on a table and
they are easy to make. Fold the paper and cut—and the
children stand in a line, hand-in-hand.

41

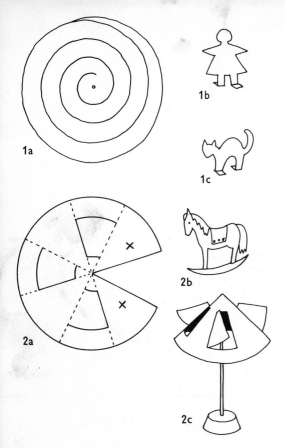

1a

1b

1c

2a

2b

2c

HEATMOBILES

When it's cold outside, and you're enjoying the warm indoors, try making a *heatmobile*. You can place one over a radiator or a heater, and the warm air currents will move it gently.

Here are two different types of heatmobiles. Both are made from thin oak tag, and both are cut from a circle. Drawing 1a shows how to cut the spiral. The small figures are cut separately and the legs have been snipped a little way up so that you can glue one leg just ahead of the other and the figure will keep its balance (1b-c). There is a small hole in the middle of the circle, where you can insert the point of a knitting needle. The mobile should just perch on the needle so that it is free to turn with the slightest movement of warm air. You can insert the other end of the needle in a potato, covered with aluminum foil, or in a large cork or a wooden block.

The *carousel* mobile is made from a circle too (2a). The circle is divided into 8 equal pieces, and one of the pieces is cut out. Then the circle is glued, one piece marked x over the other piece marked x, leaving a cone divided in 6 parts. Three of these are cut as shown in the drawings, and the carousel is placed on top of a knitting needle in the same manner as the spiral mobile. The little horses or other figures—birds, airplanes, men, women, animals—can be hung on it with a thread. If the mobile topples to one side, the balance is wrong and you must move the figures along the edge until the mobile turns around evenly.

The carousel turns round and round. The warmer it is, the
faster the horses run.

Instead of setting this on a knitting
needle, you can hang the carousel from the ceiling, where it will turn realistically.

The spiral mobile is an old familiar one,
but still it remains new and fascinating. When
you begin watching it, it's hard to turn away
again. And it's simple to make!

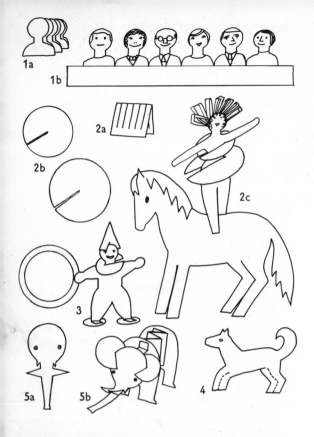

LAST OF ALL A CIRCUS

Since it's always fun to go to the circus, why not make a self-styled circus in your own living room? You can have strong men, beautiful ladies, tame pigeons and wild lions, bareback riders, small clowns—all the circus characters.

Here are suggestions for different techniques. Then you can go on playing yourself, changing the old, creating the new, as it suits you. Everything in these pictures is made from thin oak tag. The horse requires little effort; you make it stand by cutting up between the legs and spreading them slightly apart. This technique is suitable for almost all animals and people, as long as the legs are not cut too thin (2c).

The *lady bareback rider* is cut in the same way, except that she is made more elegant with her fine clothes. The clothes are made from circles of oak tag as seen in Figure 2b. The circles are slit to the center and slipped onto her body. You can see this easily in figure 2c. The *clown* and the *dog* are just as simple to make.

The *audience* is made from a series cutting and glued on a strip of oak tag curved like part of a circus ring (1a-b).

The *elephant* consists of a flat head and front and back legs held together with a Jacob's ladder fold (see page 20). The *ears* are circles slit to the center and slipped over the head. The *tusks* are cut in one piece with the head and curled gently upward (5a-b).

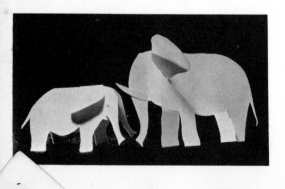

Almost anything can happen in a circus. There are limitless possibilities in shape, color, and combination. One of the elephants pictured on the opposite page is made partly with a double cutting, and one is made from a single sheet of oak tag, with the legs bent apart. The ears are drawn through a slit in the head. The lady rider's hair and the horse's plume are cut like Figure 2a. The clown and the dog you can see clearly in Drawings 3 and 4.

WHAT SHALL YOU USE TO PLAY WITH PAPER?

You can use any kind of paper. Anything from thin tissue paper to heavy tag board will do. You might use craft paper (particularly good for backgrounds), construction paper, newsprint, wax paper, silhouette paper, paper napkins, shelf paper, flint paper, tracing paper, freezer paper, wrapping paper, or Bristol board in various thicknesses.

Besides paper you will usually need a scissors. What kind of scissors depends upon who is going to use them and what they want to make. An ordinary scissors can be used for most paper cutting. If a small child is to do the cutting he should use a scissors with blunt ends. But give him *good* scissors, ones that really can cut! They are more expensive than the so-called "children's scissors" but they are more durable and much better to work with. If you want to cut something especially fine, a good embroidery scissors is excellent. For silhouettes and other cutting, which require very sharp points, it is advisable to use a special silhouette scissors.

Then there is the question of an adhesive. Flour paste is a good adhesive and it is easily available. You make it by adding 1/3 part flour to 2/3 part cold water. Make sure there are no lumps in the mixture and then bring it to a full boil as you continue beating. Most book and stationery stores, as well as drugstores and supermarkets have a good selection of adhesives.

If you don't have any paste or glue in the house, however, a cut, cooked potato can be used.

It adheres very well. Egg whites work well, too.

Gluing itself is best done in the following way: lay the pieces to be glued face down on a paper (newspaper, for example). With a brush or your fingers spread the glue or paste in a thin layer. Then place the pieces on the background with the right side up. Finally, use a clean cloth to press the pieces down and wipe away excess glue. Clothespins will hold the heavy pieces in place until the glue is completely dry. If you are working with flat pieces of heavy oak tag, it's best to press them awhile after they are glued. They will stay in place better, and you avoid puckering the oak tag.

When glossy and tissue papers are dampened on the right side, their colors tend to run. Therefore, be particularly careful not to put too much glue on them and you will have no trouble with colors smearing across backgrounds.

Finally, a few words about the basic forms and various folds. Let's begin with a square. Make a diagonal fold in the paper so that the short edge coincides with the longer edge. Cut off the extra paper and when you open the triangle you will have a square (1a). Once you have a square you can make a circle. Make a diagonal fold in the square paper (1b), and fold the paper in half again, fold against fold (1c). Again fold this in half, fold against fold (1d), and once more repeat the fold. Clip off the free ends (1e) on the line of an arc, and when you open the paper you'll have a circle.

You can draw a circle, too, with a thumbtack, a pencil, and a piece of thread or string. Put the tack in the paper, and make a loop of string the same length as the radius of the desired circle. Loop the string around the tack and the pencil. Guide the pencil around the tack, pulling the string taut as you draw the circle (1f). If you need a pentagon pattern, it's easy to make with a very long strip of paper cut approximately the width you want the sides to be. Make a flat knot in the paper, and press it securely with your fist (2a). Cut off the free ends (2b) and the pentagon is finished.

Frequently you will find use for the 16 fold, and it's easy to make. Fold a square piece of paper in half, first in one direction and then in the other (3a). The two opposite edges are then folded into the center fold line (3b), so that when you open the paper it looks like 3c. Turn the paper around and fold the other two edges into the other center fold line (3d), and the square is divided into 16 small squares.

The accordion-pleated fold is simple, too. You pleat the paper by folding it back and forth over itself (4). This fold is used for series cutting among other things.

Make your folds with great accuracy. Each fold should be pressed sharply so that you can see the line when the paper is opened.

Playing with paper does not require expensive materials, much preparation, or an abundance of time. You can improvise whenever and wherever you wish. Flexible and imaginative, it will bring you and those around you hours of amusement and a sure sense of creative fun. Try it!

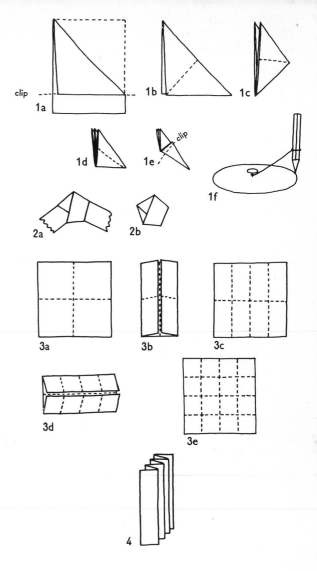

47

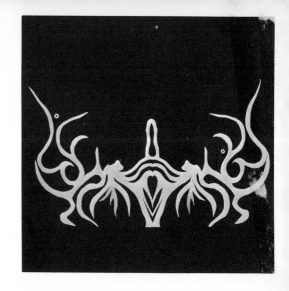

A word about adhesives:

Sobo *is an excellent adhesive. It is water soluble for cleaning purposes, and yet it dries waterproof. It is a permanent adhesive and works well on the heavier materials like oak tag and cardboard. There are other adhesives similar to it such as* Elmer's Glue.

A less expensive, but also permanent adhesive, is airplane glue. This dries too quickly, however, to allow for changes in your work. Rubber Cement *also dries very quickly, but does not adhere permanently. They both cause thinner papers to rumple.*

Mucilage *and ordinary pastes are economical, but have a number of drawbacks. They do not adhere well on heavier materials, and they will crack and dry in time. They are often messy to work with. "Roll on" (stick glues) are not satisfactory.*

48